Believe You Are Worthy

How to Transform Your Life from Self-Sabotage to Self-Mastery

Daniel Wilson

Why I wrote this book

"In the grand scheme of life", there exists a thread that holds the power to weave miracles or unravel dreams. That thread is none other than our belief in our own worthiness. It's a belief so potent, so profound, that it shapes every aspect of our existence, from the choices we make to the relationships we nurture. Yet, for many, this belief remains elusive, obscured by the shadows of doubt and self-sabotage. But fear not, for within the pages of this book lies a beacon of light, illuminating the path from self-doubt to self-mastery."

My journey as a self-help coach and personal development enthusiast has been one of profound transformation and discovery. Along the way, I've witnessed countless individuals struggle with feelings of unworthiness, trapped in a cycle of self-sabotage and stagnation. I've seen the toll it takes on their mental health, their relationships, and their overall sense of fulfillment. And through it all, I've felt a burning desire to offer them a lifeline—a roadmap to reclaiming their inherent worthiness and unlocking their limitless potential.

This book is the culmination of that desire—a testament to the power of belief and the transformative journey from self-doubt to self-mastery. It's a labor of love, born from years of experience, research, and introspection. But more than that, it's a testament to the resilience of the human spirit and the untapped potential that lies within each and every one of us.

I wrote this book because I believe, with every fiber of my being, that every individual deserves to live a life of purpose, passion, and fulfillment. I wrote it for the struggling perfectionist who longs to break free from the shackles of unrealistic expectations. I wrote it for the self-critic who yearns to silence the voices of doubt and embrace their true worth. And I wrote it for anyone who dares to dream of a better tomorrow, knowing that within them lies the power to make it a reality.

So, if you find yourself standing at the crossroads of self-doubt and possibility, unsure of which path to take, know that you are not alone. Within these pages, you'll find the guidance, the inspiration, and the tools you need to embark on a journey of profound self-discovery and transformation. Together, let us rewrite the narrative of our lives, one empowering belief at a time. Welcome to "Believe You Are Worthy"—where the journey to self-mastery begins.

How to use this book

1. **Embrace Openness and Vulnerability:** As you study each chapter, I encourage you to approach the material with an open mind and an open heart. Be willing to explore the depths of your innermost thoughts and feelings, even if it means confronting uncomfortable truths. Remember, true growth often begins at the edge of our comfort zone.

2. **Engage in Self-Reflection:** Throughout this book, you'll encounter prompts and self-reflection questions designed to deepen your understanding and facilitate personal insight. Take the time to journal your thoughts, feelings, and experiences as you work through these exercises. Allow yourself to be fully present in the moment, embracing the opportunity for self-discovery and growth.

3. **Apply What You Learn:** Knowledge without action is merely potential. As you glean insights and strategies from each chapter, commit to implementing them in your daily life. Whether it's challenging negative beliefs, practicing self-compassion, or setting meaningful goals, take deliberate steps towards embodying the principles of self-worth and self-mastery.

4. **Embrace the Journey:** Remember, transformation is not a destination but a journey—a continual process of growth and evolution. Be patient with yourself as you navigate the ups and downs of your personal development journey. Celebrate your progress, no matter how small, and trust in your ability to create positive change in your life.

5. **Seek Support and Accountability:** You don't have to walk this path alone. Reach out to friends, family members, or a trusted mentor for support and encouragement along the way. Consider joining a book club or online community where you can connect with like-minded individuals who share your goals and aspirations.

Chapter one
Understanding Self-Sabotage

Understanding self-sabotage is a vital step towards personal growth and fulfillment. It involves exploring the intricate web of thoughts, emotions, and behaviors that hinder our progress and prevent us from reaching our true potential. In this journey of self-discovery, we'll discover the roots of self-sabotage, recognize its manifestations in our lives, and unravel the psychology behind it.

The Roots of Self-Sabotage

Self-sabotage often originates from deep-seated beliefs and past experiences that shape our perceptions of ourselves and the world around us. These roots can be traced back to childhood experiences, societal influences, or traumatic events that have left an indelible mark on our psyche.

For instance, a person who grew up in a household where success was met with criticism or jealousy may internalize the belief that they are unworthy of success. This underlying belief can manifest as self-sabotaging behaviors such as procrastination, fear of failure, or avoiding opportunities for growth.

Exploring these roots requires introspection and honesty with oneself. It involves examining the narratives we've internalized about our abilities, worthiness, and potential for success. By identifying the origins of our self-sabotage, we can begin to challenge and redefine these beliefs, paving the way for positive change.

Recognizing Self-Defeating Behaviors

Self-sabotage manifests in various ways, often disguised as seemingly harmless habits or thought patterns. Recognizing these self-defeating behaviors is essential for breaking free from their grip and reclaiming control over our lives.

One common form of self-sabotage is negative self-talk, where we constantly criticize and undermine ourselves. This internal dialogue of self-doubt and self-criticism erodes our confidence and perpetuates a cycle of failure.

Another prevalent behavior is procrastination, where we delay or avoid taking action on important tasks out of fear or insecurity. Procrastination provides temporary relief from discomfort but ultimately sabotages our long-term goals and aspirations.

Additionally, self-sabotage can manifest through perfectionism, where we set unrealistic standards for ourselves and become paralyzed by the fear of falling short. This relentless pursuit of perfection not only hinders our progress but also robs us of the joy and satisfaction of achievement.

By becoming aware of these self-defeating behaviors, we can interrupt the patterns that keep us stuck and cultivate healthier alternatives. It requires mindfulness and self-compassion to recognize when we're engaging in self-sabotage and choose a different path forward.

The Psychology Behind Self-Sabotage

Understanding the psychology behind self-sabotage illuminates the underlying mechanisms driving our behaviors and thought patterns. It involves examining the interplay between our conscious intentions and subconscious beliefs, as well as the role of fear, shame, and insecurity in shaping our actions.

At its core, self-sabotage is often rooted in a fear of change or the unknown. Stepping outside of our comfort zone triggers feelings of vulnerability and uncertainty, prompting us to retreat to familiar patterns, even if they are detrimental to our growth.

Moreover, self-sabotage can serve as a misguided attempt to protect ourselves from failure or rejection. By sabotaging our efforts, we preemptively shield ourselves from the pain of disappointment or criticism, albeit at the cost of our long-term success and fulfillment.

Unraveling these psychological dynamics requires compassion and curiosity towards ourselves. It involves challenging the irrational beliefs and fears that drive our self-sabotaging behaviors and cultivating a mindset of self-acceptance and resilience.

In conclusion, understanding self-sabotage is a multifaceted journey that requires introspection, awareness, and a willingness to confront our deepest fears and insecurities. By unraveling the roots of self-sabotage, recognizing its manifestations in our lives, and understanding the psychology behind it, we can begin to break free from its grip and embark on a path of growth, fulfillment, and self-discovery.

Self-reflection questions

1. Have you taken the time to explore the underlying beliefs and past experiences that may be contributing to your self-sabotaging behaviors?

____

____

____

____

____

____

2. In what ways do you recognize self-sabotage manifesting in your life, whether through negative self-talk, procrastination, or perfectionism?

____

____

____

____

____

____

____

3. How do you respond to feelings of discomfort or vulnerability when faced with new challenges or opportunities for growth?

____

____

____

____

____

____

____

4. Are there any recurring patterns or triggers that tend to precede episodes of self-sabotage, and how can you become more mindful of these warning signs?

____

____

____

____

____

____

____

____

____

5. What steps can you take to cultivate a greater sense of self-compassion and resilience in the face of setbacks or perceived failures?

____

____

____

Chapter Two
Cultivating Self-Worth

Cultivating self-worth is a transformative journey that involves nurturing a deep sense of value and respect for oneself. In this chapter, we will explore the foundational pillars of self-worth, the power of affirmations and positive self-talk, and strategies for building confidence and competence in various aspects of life.

The Pillars of Self-Worth

Self-worth is rooted in a fundamental belief in one's inherent value and deservingness of love, respect, and fulfillment. It is cultivated through the cultivation of several key pillars that support a healthy sense of self-esteem and self-respect.

One of the foundational pillars of self-worth is self-acceptance. This involves embracing all aspects of oneself, including strengths, weaknesses, quirks, and imperfections. When we accept ourselves unconditionally, we free ourselves from the need for external validation and find inner peace and contentment.

Another essential pillar is self-awareness. Developing a deep understanding of our thoughts, emotions, and behaviors allows us to make conscious choices aligned with our values and aspirations. Through self-reflection and introspection, we can uncover our true desires and live authentically.

Additionally, self-compassion is a vital component of self-worth. Treating ourselves with kindness, understanding, and forgiveness fosters resilience in the face of challenges and setbacks. By offering ourselves the same compassion we would extend to a friend, we cultivate a nurturing and supportive inner dialogue.

Finally, self-respect is integral to cultivating self-worth. Setting boundaries, honoring our needs and desires, and advocating for ourselves empower us to create a life that aligns with our values and priorities. When we prioritize self-respect, we demonstrate to others that we are worthy of respect and consideration.

Affirmations and Self-Talk

Affirmations and positive self-talk are powerful tools for nurturing self-worth and fostering a positive mindset. Affirmations are positive statements that affirm our worth, capabilities, and potential. By repeating affirmations regularly, we can reprogram our subconscious mind and cultivate a more empowering belief system.

For example, affirmations such as "I am worthy of love and respect," "I believe in my abilities to overcome challenges," and "I deserve success and happiness" can counteract negative self-talk and reinforce a sense of self-worth.

Positive self-talk involves consciously reframing negative thoughts and beliefs into more empowering narratives. Instead of criticizing ourselves for perceived shortcomings or failures, we can choose to focus on our strengths, accomplishments, and growth opportunities.

For instance, rather than saying "I'm not good enough," we can reframe it as "I am continuously growing and learning." By shifting our self-talk from self-criticism to self-compassion, we create space for self-acceptance and personal growth.

Building Confidence and Competence

Confidence and competence are interconnected aspects of self-worth that can be cultivated through intentional practice and experience. Confidence is the belief in one's abilities to succeed in various endeavors, while competence is the actual skill and proficiency in performing tasks.

Building confidence involves stepping outside of our comfort zone and taking calculated risks. By challenging ourselves to try new things and confront our fears, we expand our comfort zone and build resilience in the face of uncertainty.

For example, if public speaking makes you feel anxious, volunteering to speak at a local event or joining a public speaking club can help build confidence and competence in this area.

Additionally, competence is developed through deliberate practice and continuous learning. By setting achievable goals, seeking feedback, and honing our skills, we gradually increase our proficiency and confidence in various domains.

For instance, if you aspire to become a better writer, committing to writing regularly, studying writing techniques, and seeking feedback from mentors or peers can help improve your competence and confidence in this craft.

In conclusion, cultivating self-worth is a journey of self-discovery and empowerment that requires nurturing the pillars of self-acceptance, self-awareness, self-compassion, and self-respect. Through affirmations and positive self-talk, we can reprogram our subconscious mind and reinforce empowering beliefs about ourselves. By building confidence and competence through intentional practice and experience, we can unlock our full potential and live a life of fulfillment and purpose.

Self-reflection questions

1. Have you taken the time to reflect on the pillars of self-worth, such as self-acceptance, self-awareness, self-compassion, and self-respect, and how they influence your sense of worthiness?

____

____

____

____

____

____

____

____

____

2. How do you incorporate affirmations and positive self-talk into your daily routine to nurture a positive mindset and reinforce beliefs in your abilities and worthiness?

3. In what areas of your life do you feel confident and competent, and how have you cultivated these qualities through deliberate practice and experience?

4. Are there any negative self-talk patterns or limiting beliefs that you have identified, and what steps are you taking to challenge and reframe them into more empowering narratives?

5. How do you prioritize self-care and self-respect in your daily life, including setting boundaries, honoring your needs and desires, and advocating for yourself in relationships and situations?

____

____

____

____

____

____

____

____

____

____

____

Chapter Three
Strategies for Self-Mastery

In the journey towards self-mastery, individuals embark on a path of personal growth and development, seeking to harness their inner potential and cultivate a sense of mastery over their lives. In this chapter, we will explore practical strategies for setting and achieving goals, overcoming procrastination and inaction, and embracing change with resilience and adaptability.

Goal Setting and Personal Vision

Goal setting is a cornerstone of self-mastery, providing a roadmap for personal and professional growth and guiding individuals towards their desired outcomes. At its core, goal setting involves clarifying one's values, aspirations, and priorities, and translating them into actionable steps and milestones.

Developing a personal vision is the first step in the goal-setting process, as it provides a clear direction and purpose for one's actions. A personal vision encompasses the ideals, dreams, and aspirations that individuals strive to manifest in their lives, serving as a guiding light and source of motivation.

For example, a personal vision might involve achieving career success, fostering meaningful relationships, or making a positive impact in the community. By articulating their personal vision, individuals can align their goals and actions with their core values and aspirations, increasing their sense of purpose and fulfillment.

Setting SMART goals is a practical strategy for translating personal vision into actionable steps and measurable outcomes. SMART goals are Specific, Measurable, Achievable, Relevant, and Time-bound, providing a clear framework for goal setting and tracking progress.

For instance, instead of setting a vague goal like "get in shape," a SMART goal might be "run a 5k race in under 30 minutes within six months," which is specific, measurable, achievable, relevant, and time-bound.

Overcoming Procrastination and Inaction

Procrastination and inaction are common obstacles on the path to self-mastery, hindering progress and sabotaging efforts to achieve goals and aspirations. Procrastination often stems from fear of failure, perfectionism, or a lack of clarity and motivation.

To overcome procrastination, individuals can employ various strategies to increase motivation and productivity. Breaking tasks into smaller, more manageable steps can help reduce feelings of overwhelm and inertia, making it easier to get started and stay focused.

Additionally, creating a conducive environment for work and minimizing distractions can help individuals maintain momentum and stay on track with their goals. This might involve setting aside dedicated time for focused work, decluttering workspaces, and limiting access to digital distractions.

Moreover, reframing procrastination as an opportunity for self-awareness and growth can help individuals understand the underlying reasons behind their procrastination and develop strategies to address them. By practicing self-compassion and cultivating a growth mindset, individuals can overcome perfectionism and fear of failure and embrace imperfection and progress.

Embracing Change and Resilience

Change is an inevitable part of life, presenting both opportunities and challenges for personal growth and development. Embracing change with resilience and adaptability allows individuals to navigate transitions and challenges with grace and confidence, fostering a sense of mastery over their lives.

Resilience is the ability to bounce back from adversity and setbacks, demonstrating flexibility and perseverance in the face of challenges. Building resilience involves cultivating coping strategies, fostering social support networks, and reframing adversity as an opportunity for growth and learning.

For example, during times of uncertainty or change, individuals can practice self-care techniques such as mindfulness, meditation, and exercise to reduce stress and enhance resilience. Seeking support from friends, family, or a therapist can also provide valuable perspective and encouragement during challenging times.

Moreover, embracing change requires a willingness to step outside of one's comfort zone and embrace the unknown. By reframing change as an opportunity for growth and self-discovery, individuals can approach new experiences with curiosity and openness, rather than fear and resistance.

In conclusion, strategies for self-mastery empower individuals to take control of their lives and cultivate a sense of purpose, resilience, and fulfillment. By setting clear goals aligned with their personal vision, overcoming procrastination and inaction, and embracing change with resilience and adaptability, individuals can unlock their full potential and achieve mastery over their lives.

Self-reflection questions

1. Have you taken the time to reflect on your personal vision and goals, considering whether they align with your values, aspirations, and priorities?

____

____

____

____

____

____

____

____

2. How do you recognize and address patterns of procrastination and inaction in your life, and what strategies have you found effective in overcoming these obstacles to progress?

____

____

____

____

____

____

____

____

3. In what ways do you approach change with resilience and adaptability, recognizing it as an opportunity for growth and self-discovery rather than a source of fear or resistance?

____

____

____

____

____

____

____

____

4. What steps are you taking to cultivate resilience and coping strategies that empower you to bounce back from adversity and setbacks with grace and confidence?

____

____

____

____

____

____

____

____

____

5. How do you integrate feedback and reflection into your journey of self-mastery, continuously refining your goals and strategies to align with your evolving vision of success and fulfillment?

____

____

____

____

____

____

____

____

____

____

Chapter four

Maintaining Your Transformation

Maintaining your transformation is an ongoing journey of growth and self-discovery that requires commitment, consistency, and resilience. In this chapter, we will explore practical strategies for cultivating daily habits that support long-term success, nurturing supportive relationships, and staying true to your path amidst life's challenges and distractions.

Daily Habits for Long-Term Success

Daily habits are the building blocks of long-term success, shaping your behaviors, mindset, and overall well-being. By incorporating intentional habits into your daily routine, you can create a foundation for sustained growth and achievement.

One essential daily habit is starting your day with intentionality. Setting aside time each morning for reflection, goal-setting, and planning allows you to align your actions with your values and priorities for the day ahead. Whether it's through journaling, meditation, or simply taking a few moments to breathe and center yourself, beginning your day with purpose sets a positive tone for the rest of the day.

Another important daily habit is maintaining a healthy lifestyle. Prioritizing activities such as regular exercise, nutritious eating, and adequate sleep not only enhances your physical health but also boosts your energy levels, mood, and cognitive function. By prioritizing self-care and well-being, you lay the groundwork for sustained success in all areas of your life.

Additionally, incorporating habits that foster personal growth and development is crucial for long-term success. Whether it's reading, learning a new skill, or engaging in creative pursuits, dedicating time each day to personal enrichment stimulates your mind, expands your horizons, and cultivates a growth mindset.

Moreover, practicing gratitude and positivity on a daily basis can have profound effects on your overall well-being and success. Taking time each day to acknowledge and appreciate the blessings in your life fosters a sense of abundance, resilience, and optimism, even in the face of challenges.

Nurturing Supportive Relationships

Supportive relationships are essential for maintaining your transformation and navigating life's ups and downs with grace and resilience. Surrounding yourself with people who uplift and inspire you, and who share your values and aspirations, provides a valuable source of support, encouragement, and companionship on your journey.

One way to nurture supportive relationships is by investing time and effort into building and maintaining connections with loved ones. Whether it's through regular communication, quality time spent together, or acts of kindness and appreciation, cultivating strong relationships requires intentionality and effort.

Additionally, practicing empathy and active listening in your interactions with others fosters deeper understanding, connection, and trust. By truly listening to others' perspectives, validating their experiences, and offering empathy and support, you strengthen your bonds and create a supportive environment where everyone feels seen, heard, and valued.

Furthermore, setting boundaries and prioritizing self-respect in your relationships is essential for maintaining your well-being and personal integrity. By communicating your needs, limits, and expectations openly and assertively, you create healthy, balanced relationships based on mutual respect, trust, and understanding.

Staying True to Your Path

Staying true to your path amidst life's distractions and challenges requires courage, resilience, and self-awareness. It involves honoring your values, aspirations, and inner guidance, even when faced with uncertainty, criticism, or setbacks.

One way to stay true to your path is by practicing self-reflection and introspection regularly. Taking time to check in with yourself, assess your progress, and realign your actions with your values and goals allows you to stay grounded and focused amidst life's twists and turns.

Additionally, cultivating mindfulness and presence in your daily life can help you stay centered and attuned to your inner wisdom and intuition. By cultivating awareness of your thoughts, emotions, and behaviors in the present moment, you can make conscious choices that honor your truth and lead you towards fulfillment and authenticity.

Moreover, embracing vulnerability and imperfection is essential for staying true to your path. Rather than striving for perfection or seeking approval from others, embracing vulnerability allows you to authentically express yourself and navigate life's challenges with courage and authenticity. By embracing your flaws and embracing vulnerability, you open yourself up to deeper connections, growth, and self-discovery. This acceptance of imperfection is a cornerstone of maintaining your transformation and staying true to your unique journey.

Self-reflection questions

1. Have you taken the time to assess the daily habits and routines that contribute to your long-term success and well-being, and are there any adjustments you can make to better support your growth and transformation?

____

____

____

____

____

____

____

____

____

2. How do you nurture and prioritize supportive relationships in your life, and how do these connections contribute to your sense of fulfillment, resilience, and personal growth?

3. In what ways do you stay aligned with your values, aspirations, and inner guidance amidst life's distractions and challenges, and how do you cultivate authenticity and integrity in your actions and decisions?

---

4. What role does self-awareness and self-reflection play in your journey of personal transformation, and how do you regularly check in with yourself to assess your progress, challenges, and areas for growth?

---

5. How do you approach vulnerability and imperfection in your life, and how does embracing these qualities contribute to your authenticity, resilience, and capacity for self-compassion and growth?

____

____

____

____

____

____

____

____

____

Conclusion

As we conclude this journey together, it's essential to take a moment to reflect on the growth you've experienced and to consider how you will continue your journey of self-mastery moving forward. Throughout our exploration of practical strategies and insights, you've gained valuable tools and perspectives to support your ongoing personal development. Now, let's delve into the importance of reflecting on your growth and embracing the continuation of your journey toward self-mastery.

Reflecting on Growth

Reflecting on your growth allows you to acknowledge and celebrate the progress you've made on your journey of self-mastery. It provides an opportunity to pause and appreciate the insights gained, challenges overcome, and lessons learned along the way. By taking stock of your achievements and areas for growth, you can cultivate gratitude for how far you've come and motivation for the road ahead.

Consider the moments of clarity and self-awareness you've experienced during this journey. Perhaps you've discovered new strengths within yourself or gained a deeper understanding of your values and aspirations. Reflecting on these insights can empower you to make intentional choices aligned with your authentic self and aspirations for the future.

Moreover, reflecting on your growth allows you to recognize and appreciate the resilience you've demonstrated in the face of challenges and setbacks. Life is full of twists and turns, and navigating them with grace and resilience is a testament to your inner strength and determination. By acknowledging the obstacles you've overcome and the lessons you've learned, you can cultivate a sense of empowerment and confidence in your ability to overcome future challenges.

Continuing Your Journey of Self-Mastery

While this chapter may mark the end of our formal exploration, your journey of self-mastery is far from over. It is a lifelong journey of growth, learning, and self-discovery that continues to unfold with each passing day. As you move forward, consider how you will continue to cultivate the habits, mindset, and relationships that support your ongoing personal development.

One way to continue your journey of self-mastery is by remaining open to new experiences and opportunities for growth. Life is filled with endless possibilities for learning and expansion, and embracing these opportunities allows you to deepen your understanding of yourself and the world around you. Whether it's trying new hobbies, exploring different perspectives, or taking on new challenges, staying curious and open-minded is essential for continued growth and self-discovery.

Additionally, prioritizing self-care and well-being is crucial for sustaining your journey of self-mastery. Taking care of your physical, emotional, and mental health allows you to show up as your best self and navigate life's challenges with resilience and grace. Whether it's through regular exercise, mindfulness practices, or seeking support from loved ones or professionals, investing in your well-being is an essential component of continued growth and fulfillment.

Furthermore, nurturing supportive relationships is vital for sustaining your journey of self-mastery. Surrounding yourself with people who uplift and inspire you, and who share your values and aspirations, provides a valuable source of encouragement, accountability, and companionship on your journey. By cultivating meaningful connections and fostering a supportive community, you create a foundation for continued growth and personal transformation.

Reflecting on your growth and embracing the continuation of your journey of self-mastery are essential steps in your ongoing personal development. By acknowledging your achievements, challenges, and lessons learned, you can cultivate gratitude, resilience, and motivation for the road ahead. As you continue your journey, remember to remain open to new experiences, prioritize self-care and well-being, and nurture supportive relationships that uplift and inspire you. With dedication, intentionality, and resilience, your journey of self-mastery will continue to unfold, leading you towards a life of fulfillment, authenticity, and purpose.

THE END